CONTENTS

V

AUTHORS AND ARTIST
Bibliography and photos of authors and artist

Peter Rossdale:
Married to Mary, nēe Lawence, who was born in Saltburn and raised in Eston, North Yorkshire. Retired veterinarian , founder of the practice Rossdale and Partners in Newmarket. Emeritus editor Equine Veterinary Journal.

Julie Galliard : Studied in London and has been involved with education - as a teacher, consultant and writer - for many years. Retirement drew her back to her native Yorkshire; she now lives in a coastal village close to Whitby which affords access to the wonderful scenery and remarkable history of this part of north Yorkshire.

James Power worked in the horse racing industry for nearly 50 years. He retired in September 2011 and has extended his lifelong talent for painting into the role of professional artist. He works in all the mediums, and covers a range of subject matters. James is an active member of the executive of the Society of Equestrian Artists (jamespowerartist@gmail.com).

With best wishes,
Julie A C Galliard 2018.

FRONT COVER
From left to right:
Top row: View from east bank towards Sandsend - Looking down the 199 steps - Entrance to the harbour.
Middle row: Schoolchildren ascending steps - East bank quayside - Boat in shipyard - Caedmon's memorial.
Lower row: St Hilda's Abbey - View through window of - St Mary's church.

Author's and Publisher's Acknowledgements
We received invaluable help and advice from Rosalin Barker, Elizabeth Cheyne, Sue Pudney, members of staff at Whitby Public library, the Pannett Museum library, and the Whitby Literary and Philosophical Society. Ada Roe and her colleagues at St Mary's church gave us helpful assistance in our search for information.
The editor and staff of the Gazette welcomed inclusion of quotations from their journal. We also consulted websites for historical information including Wikipedia,Gravestonesphoto.com; and bibliographic and source documents including Whitby North Yorkshire: An extraordinary town by Rosalin Barker, George Austen: A memoir by Wilfrid Austen, Whitby Authors and their publications 670 - 1867 by Gordon Smales, Life of Mary Linskill by Cordelia Stamp, Margaret Storm Jameson: A Life by Jennifer Birkett ,The captain Cook Monument with biographical sketch of the Great Circumnavigator (Cook, Published by Horne & Son, Ye Abbey press) and Mary Linskill by Helen Tucker.

Andre Gailani of Punch Ltd supplied the image of Du Maurier's cartoon on page 12. Typesetting was completed by Paul Hammond Design & Print and the publishing process was augmented by Kirsty Hopkins. Trevor Jones of Thoroughbred photos Ltd assisted with photography of James Power's paintings.

Preface to The Power of Whitby

The idea of the book was conceived at the summit of the 199 steps leading to the Abbey and St Mary's church. The view of the harbour and the North Sea on the one side, and the historic buildings of the Abbey and the church, with its multitude of gravestones, on the other, evoke images of past and present, of history, majesty and timelessness in human relationships.

The montage on the front cover illustrates the sights on and views from the top of the 199 steps leading to St Mary's church and the Abbey.

Churchmen, authors, explorers, mariners and boat builders have provided the town with international renown-some born in the town, others attracted as settlers or visitors.

The challenge of the environment in Whitby, with its cliffs and hillsides bisected by the mouth of the river Esk flowing into the North Sea, has typified the struggles of mankind for survival in every part of the world. Storms from the sea driving the coast and causing erosion of the landscape have resulted in loss of life, buildings and bridges, besides entailing the need for fortitude of the inhabitants in order to survive.

The purpose of this book is to pay tribute, in words and pictures, to some of those who have made the port of Whitby what it has represented in the past and what it is today.

The town of Whitby has a distinguished history with its maritime, mineral and religious connections extending over many centuries. The earliest record of a permanent settlement was in 656 when Oswy, the Christian king of Northumbria, founded the first abbey under the abbess, Hilda. The Synod held there in 664 determined the date for celebration of Easter and established the supremacy of the church of Rome. The tower and basic structure of St Mary's church are Norman and date from the early 12th century.

The geography of the town, with its position on the eastern seaboard and at the mouth of the Esk river, has inevitably entailed the association with sea-faring folk. This is particularly evident in the graveyard where those buried include the crew of the 1861 lifeboat disaster and many other mariners lost at sea. The statue on the West Cliff in memory of James Cook bears witness to the historical connection of the town to the sea.

The statue of Captain James Cook placed upon the West Cliff. In the background, the breaking waves of the North Sea serve as reminders of challenges faced by mariners in sailing for trade or exploration and of the perils faced by fisher- and life-boat men. In the picture on the right, James Power (oil) portrays the sea pounding the east cliff below the church.

The fishing port emerged during the Middle Ages and formed the basis of important herring and whaling fleets. The swivel bridge that connects the west and east sides of the town across the harbour is a reminder of the composite needs of traders to communicate while allowing free entrance and access for ships in all weathers.

Wy.319 Headway X passing through swing bridge, December 2012.

Mineral mining has been an important contribution to the economy of Whitby. The black mineraloid jet, said to be the fossilised remains of the monkey-puzzle tree, is found in the cliffs and on the moors and beaches. The Romans are known to have mined it in the area and in Victorian times jet was brought to Whitby by pack pony to be made into decorative items. It was favoured for mourning jewellery by Queen Victoria after the death of Prince Albert.

Whitby developed as a spa town in Georgian times when three chalybeate springs were in demand for their medicinal and tonic qualities. In 1839 the Whitby and Pickering Railway connecting Whitby to Pickering, and eventually to York, was built. It played a significant part in the town's tourism. Robert Stephenson, son of George Stephenson, engineer to the Whitby and Pickering Railway, was the Conservative MP for the town (1847-1859).

The present popularity of the town rests upon its history, the topography of the landscape, with its hills and surrounding North Yorkshire moorland, and the easy access to the coastline with its busy activity of ships, sailing and fishing. There is the welcoming aroma of restaurants serving fish and crustacean of all varieties, together with hotels and guest houses, many with superb views of the sea, harbour, abbey and moorland.

The 199 Steps (The Church Stairs) were originally made from wood, constructed in the 15th century and completely renovated in 2005/06. Landings with seats were originally designed to assist coffin bearers on their journey to the cliff-top graveyard. The ascent of the steps in weather ranging from sunshine to rain, and underfoot conditions, including snow and ice, is a challenge that any visitor will recognise.

Over the centuries many folk have ascended those steps or climbed Church Lane, known locally as the Donkey Path, which probably pre-dates the stairs as it led directly up to the gatehouse of the medieval Abbey.

The graveyard of St Mary contains a kaleidoscope of human happenings, similar to those portrayed in Gray's Elegy Written in a *Country Churchyard*, completed in 1750, which embody a meditation on, and remembrance after, death. The gravestones bear witness to the diversity of life; sadly, most have lost their inscriptions, so diligently compiled but unable to withstand the ravages of the weather over time in such an environment exposed to the elements.

'Each in his cell, forever laid,
The rude forefathers of the hamlet sleep.
Some mute inglorious Milton here may rest,
Some Cromwell guiltless of his country's blood.
Hands that the rod of empire might have held
Or waked to ecstasy, the living lyre,
Their lot forbade.'
Thomas Gray (1716-1771)

The need to recognise and to record is an inherent duty and pleasure for each generation - something which seemed to draw this writer down the path towards these ends - the objective being to highlight those for whom Whitby has proved an inspiration, a nurturing environment and a final resting place together with illustrations depicting their association with Whitby and other aspects relevant to their lives.

The artist selected for this purpose was James Power. Jim has a versatile history which has included a portrait of Ian Wallace, the singer, that now hangs in the Garrick Club, landscape scenes of Suffolk, Yorkshire and Cornwall. He is an accomplished professional painter, working in oils, watercolours and pastels. He is an active member of the Society of Equestrian Artists (To the right his portrait of horses near Carcassone, France). His studies for this book are rightly vested in the title *The Power of Whitby*.

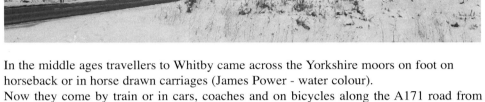

In the middle ages travellers to Whitby came across the Yorkshire moors on foot on horseback or in horse drawn carriages (James Power - water colour).

Now they come by train or in cars, coaches and on bicycles along the A171 road from Pickering.

The road to Whitby (James Power - oil).

In scanning through the content of the succeeding chapters, we hope that the reader will be enthused by glimpses provided of this historic town and by thoughts of those who lived in the past within its challenging environment; or who visited and were moved thereby to creative endeavours of writing, exploration or pious service.

A view of St Mary's church where George Austen was rector and canon for over 40 years.

25 St Hilda's Terrace - home of Reverend George Austen - viewed from Skinner Street.

CHAPTER ONE - Churchmen: The Austen family

Faith is the attribute of the mind that has acted over the eons of time as a counter to the burden of human consciousness - the burden of guilt, despair, fear - of the present and the future. Religious faith has been the predominate feature, sadly diversified into cults that vie with one another for supremacy.

Centres of Christian faith abound but Whitby has been a beacon over many centuries as witnessed by the establishment of the Abbey and its nearby church of St Mary, which provided space for prayer and meditation for those at the Abbey. The memorials and gravestones bear witness to the many churchmen who have worked in the town and devoted their lives to the people of Whitby.

The churchyard at St Mary contains the graves of George Austen and his son, George Ernest. George senior gave seventy years of service to the people of Whitby and York. His residance and place of worship shown on facing page.

Reverend George Austen

George Austen was born in 1839 into a family described by his son, Wilfrid Austen, *(George Austen: a Memoir),* as being of *'a sturdy line of Kentish Yeomen.'* He died at the age of 94 years, in August 1933, possessing mental and physical acumen into the final weeks of his life, thus anticipating the life-expectancy of the present 21st century. His life was devoted to the Church and he served in the diocese of York under five Archbishops. He was the first Vicar of St Paul's, Middlesbrough, Rector of Whitby for 45 years, Canon Residentiary of York for 25 years and Chancellor of York Minster from 1912 to 1933.

George Austen's chosen career appears to have stemmed from his entrance, in 1852, to Chatham House Academy where the headmaster, the Reverend Alfred Whitehead, father of Alfred North Whitehead, the mathematician, arranged for him to receive special tuition in Divinity. In 1858, George transferred to St John's College, Cambridge whose Master was William Bateson, the mendelian scientist who, coincidentally, was born in Whitby. At Cambridge, Austen came under the influence of Dr Vaughan, Vicar of Doncaster, when he attended a service at which the preacher invited any of those present to join him in preparation for Holy Orders.

So it was, in 1864, Austen was ordained deacon at St Mary's, Nottingham. Two years later, he was invited by the Archbishop of York, William Thompson, to become a curate in the parish of Middlesbrough. Austen, according to the memoir of his son, knew nothing of the north and had intended to return south to be near his parents. However, in 1867, he went to Middlesbrough.

His son Wilfrid recounts: *'He set himself at once to understand his surroundings and to learn about Yorkshire men. Though a Southerner himself, he had some of their distinctive characteristics. They were strong and knew how to appreciate strength in others. They were hard-headed and able to admire intellectual force in others. They had no use for weakness nor silliness; what they said they meant; and what they meant they said. In these respects Austen was one of them, although, unlike him, they could be stubborn in prejudice and distrustful of strangers. For this reason they were difficult to move and hard to win. But once won they gave their confidence and affection in full measure.'*

It was in Middlesbrough that George was introduced to Alice Agnes Abernethy, the daughter of James Abernethy, a civil engineer, who became his wife on July 26th 1873. The marriage lasted for 51 years until Alice died in 1928.

On Ascension Day 1875, Austen received an invitation from the Archbishop to become Rector of Whitby - *'a place,'* the Archbishop declared, *'which has given me more trouble than any other in my Diocese.'* Thus began, for Austen, the affection and fondness for the town and its people that lasted for more than half a century, and which ended only in his last conscious moments when he expressed the wish to be buried in the graveyard of St Mary's - the ancient church which has stood watching for centuries over Whitby and its inhabitants.

DOMESTIC ECONOMY.

Cook (to Vicar's Wife). "AND WHAT'S TO BE DONE WIIH THE SOLE
THAT WAS SAVED YESTERDAY, MA'AM?"

George du Maurier, the author and illustrator of Punch, was a frequent visitor to Whitby. He and the Rector were good friends for many years. Wilfrid Austen recalls that on one occasion his father and George were discussing religion. Du Maurier was an agnostic and Austen, with a compunction for the direct approach, made the accusation *'You are a thief, sir. You are trying to rob me of my Saviour.'* Du Maurier remembered the words - one of the characters in his novel *Trilby* utters the same phrases.

Du Maurier presented a cartoon in the September 23rd 1875 issue of Punch depicting Mrs Austen and her cook who was enquiring, *'What's to be done with the sole that was saved yesterday, m'm?'* (It is said that puns of sole and soul were popular at the time).

Du Maurier was often seen in Whitby with his lovable family pet, Chang, a St. Bernard. The dog often appeared in his Punch cartoons and became a special favourite of readers. Like Du Maurier himself, the readership was stricken when the great dog died in 1883.

The sermons preached by George Austen became something of a legend. They were based upon biblical quotations, much to the point, but including moments of humour. His sermon of Candlemas Day - February 2nd 1919 - preached at York Minster, quoted from *Exodus 3 verse 2: 'There the angel of the Lord appeared to him in flames of fire from within a bush. Moses saw that though the bush was on fire it did not burn up.'*

York Minster with Lendal Bridge in the foreground (James Power - oil).

Why, asked the Dean, did the bush keep burning? Because the Lord was there and he spoke out of it, while God's people laboured in the midst of Egyptian bondage. This led into the subject of the sermon, namely the fires that had occurred at the Minster - the great fire of 741, another on September 19th 1069, resulting from the fight between the English, Scots and Danes and yet another in 1189 when citizens who had borrowed money from the Jews broke open chests where bonds of debt were deposited and set fire to them. In 1216 the torch of a careless watchman set fire to the city and the Minster, and in 1753 an injudicious workman set fire to the roof.

Perhaps the most intriguing account of a Minster fire was that of 1829 when, on Candlemas Day, the choir stall was set alight by the fanatic, Jonathan Martin, who had had two dreams which he took to be *'the will of God.'* Jonathan had written five letters to members of the clergy complaining about their policies. He was incensed when he received no reply. He attended Sunday evening service to which was added 'the buzz' of the organ about which he exclaimed *'Thou shalt buzz no more. I will burn thee down tonight.'*

He hid behind Archbishop Greenfield's tomb in the North Transcript and waited until the bell-ringers had left. Entering their chamber, he cut off 80 feet of rope to make a scaling ladder and climbed across to the choir stall. He piled up prayer books and cushions and set light to them with candles before escaping via the Five Sisters' window.

As the clock struck 3am, a chorister named Swinbank, slipped on the ice in the city. As he lay on his back, he saw smoke issuing from the roof of the Minster. He gave the alarm and all the fire-engines of York arrived. The organ had caught fire and the action of heated air in the pipes *'caused an awe-inspiring noise which echoed through the building.'*

By 9am, all the choir was ablaze. The roof began to fall, with molten lead pouring down in torrents; two hours later it had collapsed. In early afternoon, the fire subsided but the pulpit, choir and Lady Chapel were destroyed along with many tombs and monuments.

Martin was apprehended and tried at Leeds assizes where he was defended by Brougham, afterwards Lord Chancellor. He was found guilty but insane and ended his days in Betlehem Hospital.

In 1840 misfortune struck the Nave and Southwest Tower of the Minster. They burned down after a clockmaker left his lighted candle in a flat piece of wood when he finished work. The fire-engines arrived to find there was no water and by midnight the flames reached the great central tower. The scene was described as one of *'awful magnificence'* and was visible as far away as Harrogate.

Austen concluded his Candlemas Day sermon: *'And so our Cathedral, in spite of all changes wrought by successive foes, stands unconsumed like the burning bush - proclaiming that God is in our midst.'*

On the 3rd July 1921, Austen again preached about the Minster. He spoke of *'Our holy and beautiful house'* and quoted the poet Canon Richard Wilton:

> *'With wondering eyes we sit and gaze*
> *Upon the many-jewelled blaze,*
> *Where art flung her mighty dyes.'*

He referred to the Great East Window as composed of three contrasting shades of colour - the darker shade of the lower part with the light blue tints above which speak to us of the sky, and, above all, the pure white tints which speak to us of heaven and its holiness. He claimed that *'In no Cathedral of the world can we see such a variety of windows of every shade and shape.'*

On 25th June 1925, Austen delivered a sermon which is relevant to the controversy of today concerning women's roles in the church. This was based upon St Luke, chapter 8, verses 2 and 3: *'Certain women who ministered unto him.'* In the course of the sermon Austen observed *'Women are peculiarly endowed with gifts and graces that fit them for the work of ministry.'*

The choir stalls in York Minster where Jonathan Martin's fire began (James Power - oil).

Austen died in York on August 3rd 1933. Three days later, his body was transported to Whitby where his coffin was carried up the 199 steps to be interred at the entrance to the churchyard - the place he had chosen for his grave many years previously. Canon Sykes conducted his funeral, concluding with the words: *'The long day closes and now his earthly remains are brought to be laid among his own people and in the place where his heart has been for more than half a century.*

George Ernst Vaughan Austen

An obituary appeared in the Whitby Gazette, dated 23.08.1907: *'It is with regret that we record the death of Mr George Ernest Vaughan Austen, eldest son of the Rev. Canon Austen, M.A., Rector of Whitby, which sad event took place on Tuesday. The deceased underwent an operation for embolism at Guy's Hospital, London, and was thought to be recovering nicely, when he suddenly succumbed. He was born in 1874, and was educated privately, and at the late Mr H Hallgate's Spring Hill School. He gained a scholarship at Winchester and went from there to New College, Oxford, where he graduated as M.A; proximi accessit, Hertford; first-class moderating. He was classical master at Queen Elizabeth's College, and up to the time of his death had been scholarship master at King's School, Canterbury, for six years. He was the joint editor of 'Theophrastus.' The deceased had taken an active part in the social life of the town, and its sports. Much sympathy is expressed towards Canon and Mrs Austen in their bereavement.'*

There can be no doubt that the son inherited his father's intelligence, although sadly not his longevity of life.

Wilfrid Abernethy Evers Austen

Wilfrid was his father's biographer; he remained true to his father's ideals as shown by two books he authored, namely: *A Popular Guide to the Structure and Endowments of the Church of England and to the Solution of the Problem of Voluntary Offerings* and *The Structure and Endowments of the Church of England: A Popular Guide* published by the Society for Promoting Christian Knowledge both published in the 1920s.

Pastel sketch by James Power of Austen based upon portrait in the memoir written by his son Wilfrid and published by Horne and Son Ltd. The colours of his sash represent Whitby Town coat of arms, White Rose of Yorkshire, blue band for the sea and white cross for St George.

CHAPTER TWO - Writers

The profession of writer and authorship is as old as mankind's ability to possess conscious thought and language. Authorship is the art of committing the thoughts of an individual into print or, nowadays, by means of the many routes of communication online.

What drives an individual to write is a personal motivation with a multitude of different viewpoints extending over early life and continuing as the writer becomes older. In particular the circumstances of birth and childhood, together with experiences encountered in day-to-day existence, are paramount - all molded by the genetic character of the individual.

Whitby has acted as an incentive to writers, to record facts and as a spur to their imagination, as it has to artists and churchmen. Gideon Smales in the book *Whitby Authors and their Publications 670-1867,* published by Horne and Sons in April 1867, lists nineteen authors described as poet, philosopher, historian, arctic explorer and circumnavigator. Caedmon, the illiterate shepherd who dreamt the poetry now celebrated as Caedmon's hymn, is commemorated in St Mary's churchyard with the inscription: *'To the glory of God and in memory of Cædmon the father of English Sacred Song. Fell asleep hard by in the year 680.'*

View of the Caedmon Memorial.

Caedmon was the English poet who cared for the animals at the monastery of Streonæshalch now known as Whitby Abbey during the abbacy of St. Hilda (657-680). He learned to compose one night in the course of a dream, according to the 8th century monk, Bede. He later became a zealous monk and an inspirational Christian poet.

This chapter considers the effects of Whitby upon two writers born in the town - Mary Linskill and Margaret Storm Jameson and three other authors who gathered inspiration *en passant,* so to speak, namely Elizabeth Gaskell, Lewis Carroll and Bram Stoker.

Artist's concept of Hild's nuns of the monastery singing Caedmon's Hymn (James Power - oil).

Mary Linskill

Mary Linskill was born on December 13th 1840 in a cottage in Blackburn's Yard, one above some twelve other houses in the yard, mostly occupied by mariners. Mary's father, Tom was a watchmaker later becoming a constable, one of three in the town.

Memorial to Linskill in Blackburn Yard.

Looking into the Yard from Church Street.

Looking into the Yard from Church Street.

Views of Blackburn Yard leading into Church Street.

In Mary's day the Yard would have been noisy with the sounds of hammering from the shipyard nearby and shouts from multitudes of children of all ages playing. As the eldest child, Mary was relied upon by her mother to help with domestic chores and the care of her younger siblings. The death of her favourite brother Thomas when she was nine, then, two weeks later, the death of her two year old brother James, affected Mary badly - she would wander the churchyard listening for the voices of her two brothers carrying on the wind. Thanks to her father's position, Mary, intelligent and solitary, was educated in a private local academy which enabled her to secure a position as an apprentice milliner with Charles Wilson who had business premises at the lower end of Bridge Street, training which eventually led her to Newcastle-under-Lyme and a position as Head Milliner.

Never happy in her career, Linskill took a teaching post in a small school before working as a governess in Derby. In poor health and longing for the bracing air and rugged scenery, Linskill returned home to Whitby where she met the Lupton family from Leeds. They became good friends who supported and encouraged her writing - her stay with them in Leeds coincided with her first published work *Tales of the North Riding* (1871) for which she used the pseudonym Stephen Yorke.

The heather (courtesy of Jennie Evans) and the north sea - sights and sounds which fuelled Mary Linskill's creative imagination.

Linskill continued to write - her inspiration, as with other famous writers, evolved from the contrasts within her life and her feelings for her native town: '*A beautiful place to have been born in, beautiful with history and poetry and legend - with all manner of memorable and soul-stirring things.*' *(The Diary of Mary Linskill)*. She sought refuge in the creative endeavours of writing in terms both of imagination and fact - a form perhaps of escapism - as she suffered continually from bouts of depression, not helped by the situation at home where her younger sister, Emma, the spoilt youngest child left at home, ruled the household causing tensions between the two sisters.

With the sudden death of her father, and news of his disastrous investments, Linskill's life changed for the worse as lack of money to pay household bills and buy food reduced her to borrowing money from friends and neighbours. Her state of mind became increasingly precarious and she turned to laudanum to try to combat her chronic insomnia and melancholic fears. Her writing earned only a meagre income. The poor health of her sister Emma and with her mother also failing, Linskill was prompted to take a cottage in Newholm, hoping the peace and tranquillity of country life would bring healing but it was not to be. Medical treatments and nursing depleted already dwindling savings and relationships deteriorated further before Emma went to live with other relatives.

Even as penury threatened the class conscious Victorian society recognised Linskill's literary achievements and elevated her to the circles of the social elite. Not wanting to lose this status, Linskill fought in vain against returning to live in the lowly yards of Whitby, but her diary entry for 1877 shows how desperate she was feeling:

'Every day I grow weaker, my mental energy fails. My desire for final rest grows stronger.
I have asked three of the richest people in the neighbourhood for temporary help and have
been denied by everyone of them. Two of them are women and know that I am frail in health,
and alone in the world and a member of the same Christian church as themselves. I say it in
no rebellious mood, but I feel that my gravestone would be a tender thing to lay my cheek against today.'

Too ill to write much, and unable to afford the opiates to combat her depression, Linskill suffered unimaginably...... yet she rejected a proposal of marriage from young curate, Tilden Smith. Cordelia Stamp, in her *Biography of Mary Linskill,* suggests she may have been in love with - and loved by - a married man. Passages in her writing reflect deep emotional feelings and some autobiographical detail may be reflected in the characters of Dorigen and Michael in her book *The Haven under the Hill* which gives an insight into the lives of the jet-workers and their industry. It also contains a memorable passage based on the famous lifeboat tragedy of 1861. The realistic description of the scene sounds as if she witnessed the terrible events from the pier at the time.

Despite everything, Linskill continued to write copiously, drawing on her own experience. She became a popular author with Victorian readers who enjoyed her characters and their tragic lives. However, it was the backdrop of Whitby and its dramatic surroundings that made, and still makes, her writing memorable. *Hild's Haven or Port St Hilda* - Whitby in disguise - are clearly depicted by a writer whose affection for her home town cannot be denied.

1884 brought a change in the Linskill fortunes. *Between the Heather and the Northern Sea* was serialised in the magazine Good Words and became an instant success, ensuring a wide and enthusiastic readership when it was published as a novel in 1887. The Spectator's review highlighted its descriptions of *'wild high moorland and lonely, desolate reedy marshes.'*

Success brought income and Linskill was once again able to leave Blackburn's Yard and move with her mother into a fashionable house in Spring Vale. However, her harrowing life had taken its toll and she rarely left the house. Mary Linskill died on 9th April 1891, aged 51. She was buried in Whitby Cemetery, resting in the place where, as a girl, she had wandered listening for the voices of her dead brothers.

Portraits of Mary Linskill from the story of her life by Fiona J. Mukerjee in Down Your Way magazine issue 61.

The sculptor, John Tweed, made the seven feet six inches high bronze figure of Cook on its freestone pedestal. The statue was presented to the town of Whitby by the Hon. Sir Gervase Becket, M.P. and unveiled on 2nd October 1912. It shows Cook as a navigator holding the tools of the trade he learned at Whitby - a pair of compasses and a chart. The plinth bears a model of *Resolution* one of the Whitby built ships which carried him on his voyage to the south seas.

Much has been written about Captain James Cook. Suffice it to say his epoch-making voyages of exploration provided hitherto unknown information about the lands of the southern hemisphere, and led to further exploratory missions financed by the British government. It has been said *'the map of the Pacific Ocean is the best memorial to Captain Cook.'*

Children from West Cliff Primary School joined Whitby Mayor John Freeman, Borough Mayor Helen Mallory and the Rev Canon David Smith to celebrate the 100th anniversary of the unveiling of the statue to Whitby's most famous apprentice - 2nd October 2012. Photo courtesy of the Whitby Gazette.

The inscription on the statue reads *'for the lasting memory of a great Yorkshire seaman, this Bronze has been cast, and is left in the keeping of Whitby: the Birthplace of those good ships that bore him on his Enterprises, brought him to Glory, and left him at Rest.'*

Captain William Scoresby

The Scoresby family produced two of Whitby's most famous and accomplished Captains. Captain William Scoresby, senior (1760-1829) ran away to sea and became a renowned and successful whaler and Arctic explorer while his son went to university, subsequently combining scientific study of the arctic regions with whaling before turning his back on both when he became an Anglican priest.

Whalers in the arctic circle (James Power - oil on canvas).

The Scorseby family at home and on their way to church (James Power - oil).

William Scoresby senior invented the crow's nest, a structure in the upper part of the main mast of a ship, to shelter men who spent hours at the top of the mast in freezing winds, searching for whales and looking for a channel through the dangerous ice. In early ships, it had been simply a barrel or a basket lashed to the tallest mast.

Whaling was highly dangerous but very lucrative; there was a great demand for the versatile whale products as the north-east industrialised. The majority of the whaling ships centred on Whitby and Newcastle and many fine houses were built on the proceeds of the industry.

After spending 43 years at sea he spent his retirement proposing and making improvements to Whitby. He drew up plans for the East pier and provided a water pump in Church Street - now in Pannett Park Museum - which bears a Latin inscription saying: *'Water for the free use of all. Draw and drink but don't gossip.'* His two Whitby homes survive - the red-brick Scoresby House in Church Street, and No 13, Bagdale, where he died in 1829, aged seventy-nine.

Views of 13 Bagdale from the front and from across the Quaker burial ground. There are many more interred in the cemetery than there are stones of remembrance because the Qukers did not favour gravestones. Further, they would not allow burial of mariners who had carried a gun in their lifetime.

Reverend William Scoresby (1789-1857)

William Scoresby, only son of Captain William Scoresby, was born after the family had made their fortune from Arctic whaling. He was determined to follow in his father's footsteps. As a ten year old child William junior made his first sea trip with his father after stowing away, voyaging to Greenland on board the Dundee which was threatened by French pirates and imprisoned in ice for eight weeks. At 17, he joined his father on board the whaling ship Resolution, (not to be confused with Captain Cook's ship of the same name), as chief officer. In 1811 Scoresby married the daughter of a Whitby ship builder and, in the same year, was given command of the Resolution upon his father's retirement. He was the youngest ever whaling captain, helping to bring back the biggest single catch of any Whitby ship - thirty whales.

Each voyage from Whitby saw Scoresby's observations advance scientific and geographic knowledge. On his many Arctic voyages he followed his father's example and began studying meteorology and the natural history of the polar regions. These experiences fuelled his passion for scientific studies and on his return from sea he attended natural philosophy and chemistry lectures at Edinburgh University. The papers he wrote of his observations whilst at sea ensured his election as a member of the Wernerian Natural History Society (1808-1858), an elite off-shoot of the Royal Society of Edinburgh. They were published in two volumes in 1820 entitled *Account of the Arctic Regions,* laying the foundation of modern Arctic science.

Young William Scoresby's whaling days ended in 1823, the same year he took Holy Orders and became one of the early members of the Whitby Literary and Philosophical Society formed to provide Whitby with its Museum, which still runs as an independent Museum today.

As an Anglican priest, William Scoresby junior worked first in East Yorkshire before moving to Bradford where he worked tirelessly as vicar of St Peter's - a small parish which increased to 100,000 as a result of the population explosion of the early nineteenth century. He became a vigorous social reformer - fighting hard for better sanitation and a reduction in air pollution. He also founded schools and helped to start a 'Friendly Society,' which ran its own bank and provided sickness benefits for factory girls.

It was his early religious faith, learned in Whitby where he climbed the 199 steps every Sunday to the Parish Church, that carried the younger Scoresby through many adversities. He never lost his interest in Whitby, returning to preach in the parish church when two Whitby ships were lost with considerable loss of life. It is said the congregation, on that occasion, overflowed into the churchyard.

He retired to Torquay where he died on 21st March 1857. His affection for Whitby led him to bequeath his collection of Arctic curiosities, scientific instruments and all his papers, including his ships' logs and journals to Whitby Museum. The museum also contains the younger Scoresby's compound magnetic needle that he invented as the solution to the compass problem.

In this chapter we endeavoured to provide a glimpse of those involved in the fascination of exploration and how Whitby afforded a starting place for their adventures and played a role in the spirit of their enterprises.

CHAPTER FOUR - Mariners

Whitby's position on the North Sea coastline is a natural point for seafaring activity. The entrance to, and exit from, the river Esk provides natural geography for a port and a harbour to shelter from prevailing winds. There is no evidence that the port was used by the Romans but there are mentions of Whitby fishermen in the 12th Century.

The names on gravestones and monuments of those buried in the churchyard at St Mary bear witness to the service and dedication of Whitby mariners over the past centuries - both as seamen and the subject of disasters that are inherent for those that *'Go down to the sea in ships and do business in great waters; These see the works of the Lord, and his wonders in the deep.'* There are numerous names designated as Master Mariner and some as Shipbuilder or Shipwright, buried in the cemetery, bearing witness to the spirit of the inhabitants of Whitby over the centuries.

To paraphrase the inscription on the dome of St Paul's cathedral dedicated to its architect Sir Christopher Wren *'If you want to see a monument to the spirit of Whitby folk, look around you and read the epitaphs on gravestones.'*

John Barritt, Pilot, who was drowned off Whitby December 1845 Aged 37 years.

Sir Richard Atkinson Robinson (1849 - 1928).

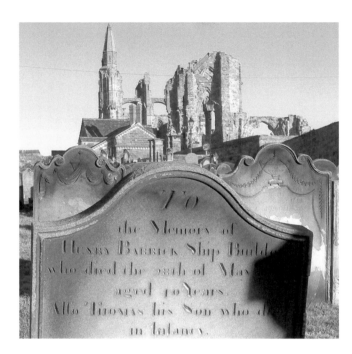

Henry Barrick ship builder died March 1797 age 40 years. Son Thomas died in infancy. Owned yard on Bagdale dock.

Many sailors died at sea, off the coast or far afield, such as Thomas Baxter *'who was killed on board HMS Scout by a shot from a Spanish gunboat off Cape Trafalgar November 2nd 1807 age 30 years'* or John Foxton *'drowned on board the Bellona near Brest January 21st 1814 age 28 years'* and Samuel Tulley *'who perished with all the crew of the King George of Whitby on their passage from New York January 2nd 1782 age 33 years.'* The last entry not referring to HMS Royal George, one of Britain's greatest and most victories warships which, in August 1782, sank when undergoing repairs at Spithead in the Solent.

Whitby mariners sailed far and wide. The Times newspaper of 30 March 1882 carried an entry which recognised the bravery of Captain William Jefferson, of the steamship Caedmon, who had been presented at Whitby with a silver medal and diploma from the King of Portugal, in recognition of *'his bravery and humanity in rescuing the crew of the Portuguese schooner, Alexander Secundo, in the Bay of Biscay in October 1881.'*

The 1861 lifeboat disaster
The 1861 lifeboat disaster represents the very essence of the term *'perils of the sea'* and provides a focus that is mirrored countless times over past centuries, and into the present day.

Example of rough seas (Gale force seven) on February 3rd 2012.

The disaster was reported in the Whitby Gazette of 16th February 1861 under the heading:

Fearful Storm.
Dreadful loss of life and shipping.

On the morning of February 9th 1861, a fierce gale was blowing, said at the time to be greater than any experienced for many years. Many vessels sought refuge on the Whitby shoreline.
At 8.30am, the Whitby lifeboat crew, including Henry Freeman, Robert Leadley, John Storr, George Martin, William Tyreman, William Dryden and John Dixon set out to rescue the crew of the John and Ann of Sunderland, floundering near Sandsend.
At 10am, the schooner Gamma of Newcastle was driven ashore about 400 yards from the Pier and the lifeboat crew rowed out for the vessel.
A Prussian Barque, The Clara of Memel, came ashore at 11.30am a little to the north of the Gamma and the lifeboat again took all the crew off. The rescue party returned, tired and hungry, placed the lifeboat onto its carriage, and took a glass of grog.
Before long, two more vessels, the brig Utility and the schooner Roe, were both seen coming ashore near the coastguard station. The lifeboat men again rowed out to save the crews 'amid the hearty congratulations of the immense concourse of spectators.'
By 12 noon the storms were relentless; both the Flora of London and the Merchant were seen in trouble by early afternoon. Flora came in beautifully but the Merchant's main mast gave way; she came ashore near the Roe so the lifeboat had to set out again to manoeuvre the vessels to avoid a collision. Suddenly 'a tremendous cross sea, passing on each side, caught the lifeboat at the stern of the vessel, turning her completely over towards the pier, and threw all her gallant crew into the foaming billows. John Storr succeeded in getting upon the bottom of the boat, and others were floating about with their lifebelts on, struggling for their lives.' Although John Storr managed to climb onto the overturned boat he was exhausted and 'was obliged to yield and perished.'

The sole survivor was Henry Freeman - the only crew member wearing a cork lifejacket. All the men had these available but had chosen different lifejackets which hung too low on their bodies, according to Captain Butler of the Coastguard station. Had they followed Freeman's example, they too would have been saved.

The men who died on the Lifeboat were:

John Storr: the Coxswain (left a widow and 1 child aged 16 years).

John Dixon: (a widow and 8 children). Robert Leadley: (a widow and 7 children).

Robert Harland: (a widow and 6 children). William Walker: (a widow and 5 children).

Isaac Dobson: (a widow and 6 children). John Philpot: (a widow and 5 children).

William Storr: (bringing up 3 children since his wife had died).

William Tyreman: (a widow and 2 children). Matthew Leadley: (a widow and 2 children).

George Martin: (a widow and a 1 month old baby). Christopher Collins: (single).

Sea raging against East Cliffs (2013) with bunch of memorial flowers in foreground; symbolic of the hymn composed by the reverend William Whiting after coming through a fierce storm. The words were coincidently written in 1860, the year before the great lifeboat disaster.
"Oh, hear us when we cry to Thee, for those in peril on the sea!"

The consequence of the disaster is neatly summed by the epitaph on the headstone dedicated to William Walker, age 59. This stone was lost in a landslide but its inscription read:

'With footsteps firm to the Pier bent his way
The tempest lashed the bitter blast
His fellow creatures' lives to save
And caused him an untimely grave.

The gradual erosion of the cemetery has resulted in those buried near the cliff edge being lost and only their tombstones being recovered. Three such stones are propped against the church wall. The two to the right of the main church entrance are those of George Martin and William Storr, while to their right is that of John Storr. The latter was described in the Whitby Gazette as *'A fine steady man, worthy of the confidence and respect which he had gained among his brother fishermen.'* Originally the stone was placed where John Storr was interred, but it was lost in a subsequent landslide onto Henrietta street. (See chapter 5).

On the 12th February 1861 a letter to the Editor appeared in The Times under the heading *'The Loss of the Whitby Lifeboat.'* This was signed by William Keane, Perpetual Curate of Whitby, and in this he claimed that those in Whitby would support the bereaved families as best they could but called upon readers of The Times to contribute. Several days later a second letter listed a number of donations including that of £5 (£210 in today's value) from one Charles L Dodgson - presumably Lewis Carroll.

Henry Freeman, the sole survivor, continued his service and was recognised by The National Lifeboat Institution, in 1880, when he was awarded their special service clasp.

Stormy sea at Sandsend
(James Power - oil).

Lifeboat in stormy seas in
early 19th century
(James Power - oil).

Henry Freeman

Henry Freeman born in Bridlington in 1835 and employed in the brick making trade before moving to Whitby and taking up seamanship. This was his first voyage with the lifeboat crew; he was the only member who was wearing the newly developed cork life jacket. He was awarded the RNLI's silver gallantry medal and served a further 40 years as a lifeboat man. He became a favourite subject of John Sutcliffe's photography and died in 1904 .

"A Victorian Photograph" by Frank Meadow Suttcliffe of Henry Freeman in his cork lifejacket, circa 1880 (By permission Suttcliffe Gallery).

Henry lived in Bakehouse Yard, a narrow turning off Cliff street that runs into Flowergate. A plaque has been placed on the entrance to the Yard. The inscription recounts how, in January 1881, he led a team that dragged the then lifeboat *"Robert Whitworth"* six miles over land from Whitby where conditions prevented launching, to Robin Hood's Bay in a blizzard, thus saving thirty one souls in the wrecked brig *"Visiter"*.

"Whitby Fishermen by the Harbour Rail" is the title of a photograph by John Sutcliffe which includes Henry Freeman (third from left) the only survivor of the 1861 disaster. (Published by permission of the Sutcliffe Gallery).